Curios

of

West Sussex

A County Guide
to the Unusual

by

David Arscott

S.B. Publications

By the same author: *The Sussex Story*
Curiosities of East Sussex
The Upstart Gardener
A Sussex Quiz Book

(with Warden Swinfen):   *Hidden Sussex*
People of Hidden Sussex
Hidden Sussex Day by Day
Hidden Sussex — The Towns

Video narration: *Discovering West Sussex*
Discovering Brighton

First published in 1993 by S.B. Publications
c/o 19 Grove Road, Seaford, East Sussex BN25 1TP.

British Library Cataloguing in Publication Data
available from the British Library on request

ISBN 1-85770-017-1

Typeset and printed by Delmar Press (Colour Printers) Ltd., Nantwich, Cheshire

CONTENTS

CONTENTS

CONTENTS

All photographs by the author.
Front Cover: ....Charles Cook gravestone at Walberton.
Title page: ....Roadside St Christopher at Treyford.
Back Cover: ....Railway carriage home at Shoreham Beach.

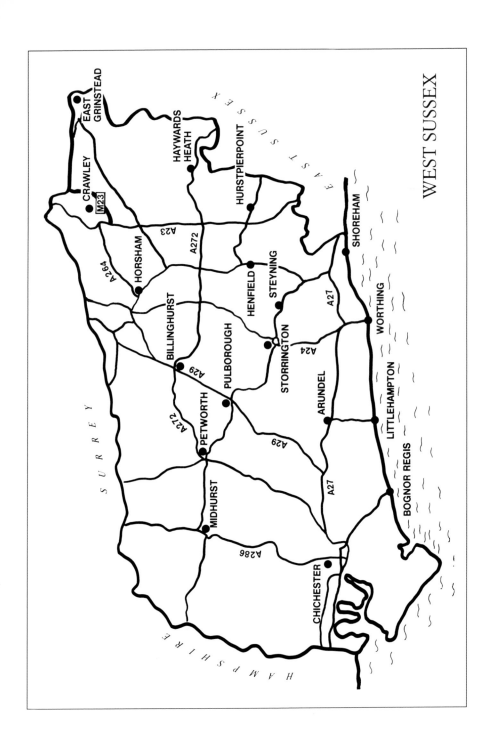

WEST SUSSEX

INTRODUCTION

The west of Sussex is rather less explored than the east. It has fewer large towns and considerably more small villages, a good many of them tucked away from the main thoroughfares. My travels in pursuit of the unusual have served not only to remind me of the west's comparative remoteness but to convince me (for an author needs to feel that his books may have some purpose other than his own amusement) that the great majority of the objects featured here will be unknown to most of my readers. I do hope you enjoy the exploration as much as I have done.

To avoid endless frustrations, you need a good map. I have used the Ordnance Survey 1:50,000 Landranger series, and given every curiosity its grid reference: not having the benefit of these 'fixes' myself cost me hours of futile, misguided traipsing. To cover every inch of Sussex I'm afraid you will need seven maps (186-189 and 197-199), but you don't, of course, have to buy them all at once.

What qualifies as a curiosity is a moot point, and I would not care to debate it. The inclusion of 'firsts' and 'only survivings' needs no apology, it seems safe to say. Colourful churchyard inscriptions are likewise impossible to ignore, and West Sussex has a good clutch of these. Follies, too: the west had no Mad Jack Fuller *(see the East Sussex volume)*, but the landscape is nevertheless scattered with decaying decorative towers. Otherwise my choice simply reflects personal taste, or lack of it, and the need for variety.

Books of local history (which this is, in part) are for some reason prone to the endless recycling of bogus 'facts'. Ghosts haunt every old building, there are hidden tunnels running from every inn, and place-names are given the silliest derivations imaginable. It would be a foolish author who claimed that his every line was free from error, but there really is no need for these tired, unimaginative fabrications. As I hope this book will show, truth itself is sufficiently curious to need no overlay of fiction.

David Arscott

This elaborate locking device on the chapel door at Sackville College (see p. 88) is still working perfectly after more than 350 years.

CHICHESTER

THE DODO HOUSE

> *Access:* Outside Pallant House, at the crossing of the four Pallants, south east of the market cross.
>
> *Map Reference:* SU863045

The wine merchant Henry 'Lisbon' Peckham, who had Pallant House built as his home and business premises in the early eighteenth century, boasted ostriches on his coat of arms and therefore ordered a couple for his gateposts. Unhappily, the poor stonemason had only drawings to go on. He'd obviously never seen an ostrich in his life, and the ungainly creatures he produced have bestowed upon this fine building (now an art gallery with an outstanding contemporary collection) the undignified nickname of 'the dodo house'.

At Parham Park near Storrington you can witness the product of a similar herculean artistic struggle against heavy odds. After Sir Joshua Reynolds brought back a kangaroo skin from Australia, George Stubbs inflated it and did his best to imagine what the living marsupial would have looked like. The result is hardly up to the standard he achieved with his pictures of horses, but it was, at least, the first painting of a kangaroo to be seen in Europe.

1

CHICHESTER

MARKET CROSS

Access: At the meeting of the city's four main thoroughfares.
Map Reference: SU861047

Alfriston's sad stump apart, this is the only surviving market cross in the whole of Sussex – but what a rich creation it is, with its ogee canopies, crocketed pinnacles and elaborate tracery overtopped by a weather-vaned cupola carried on ribbed vaulting. The octagonal cross made of Caen stone was given to the city by Edward Story, the then Bishop of Chichester, in 1501. The bronze bust of Charles the First was installed during the reign of his son, while the four clock dials were added in 1746.

BOSHAM

A SAILOR'S GRAVESTONE

Access: In the churchyard south-east of the church by the path.
Map Reference: SU804039

Poor Thomas Burrow, master of the sloop Two Brothers, has his sad end illustrated on his tombstone at Bosham. He fell into the sea and drowned on October 13, 1759, when a rope broke: the severed ends and the plummeting sailor can be clearly seen. Burrow turned his hand to smuggling but, as noted in our companion volume for East Sussex, this was no deterrent to a decent burial and a proud epitaph. In this case the sentiments are particularly high-flown:

> *Though Boreas's storms and*
> *Neptune's waves*
> *have tos'd me to and fro*
> *Yet I at length by Gods decree*
> *am harbourd here below*
> *Where at Anchor here I lay*
> *with many of our Fleet*
> *Yet once again I shall set Sail*
> *my Saviour Christ to meet*

The inscription was apparently well received. Note the remarkably similar tombstone to a sailor who died at *West Wittering* some years later.

3

BOSHAM

FLOOD BARRIERS

Access: In the streets close to the harbour.
Map Reference: SU805039

Parking your car by the water's edge at Bosham (pronounced Bozz'm) is a hazardous business but, as this picture shows, the locals are well prepared for the flooding which has always been a feature of living by a creek on the fringe of Chichester Harbour. Clambering over a barrier to get inside your house is a far better option than having your floors awash at regular intervals.

The persistent encroachment of the sea is the best explanation for the myth that King Canute ordered the waves to retreat here and that his young daughter was buried in the church. There is no convincing evidence for either event, whereas Bosham was certainly the church at which the future King Harold prayed before journeying to France and being fatally compromised by William, Duke of Normandy. The church is illustrated on the Bayeux Tapestry.

4

CHURCH NORTON

THE EARLIEST CHRISTIAN SITE IN SUSSEX

Access: Signposted off the B2145 between Sidlesham and Selsey.
Map Reference: SZ872958

This little church is near the site of the monastery founded by St. Wilfrid after he fled Northumbria in the year 681. The saint is credited not only with converting the people of Sussex to Christianity, but with teaching them to fish – surely the ultimate in fishy tales. A bishopric of Selsey was created in 709, and twenty three bishops were to hold office before the See was removed to Chichester in 1070.

What you see here is a remnant of the thirteenth century successor to Wilfrid's original church. It's a remote spot, ideal for bird-watchers but inconvenient for regular worship: in the 1860s it was decided that Selsey village needed its own church, and that the existing building at Church Norton should be demolished in order to provide the materials. Ecclesiastical law, however, forbids the removal of a chancel – which is the part that remains to this day.

GOODWOOD

MILESTONE

Access: By the roadside some 200 yards from Goodwood House.
Map Reference: SU885085

It was the third Duke of Richmond who built Goodwood House at the end of the eighteenth century, though he ran out of money before his grand design could be completed. He was, of course, much concerned with his 'prospect', and this necessitated re-routing the Petworth road. A few of the original milestones can still be seen, however, marking distances from the market cross at Chichester.

Among the features to look out for in the grounds are the old ice house, disguised as a garden pavilion within a cool copse, and a number of cork trees planted by the third Duke. On a hill behind the house the wife and daughters of the second Duke spent seven years building 'the shell house', a grotto lined with shells sent to the family by Captain Knowles of HMS Diamond and other naval officers serving overseas.

ALDSWORTH

RACTON TOWER

> *Access:* Up a track off the B2146 a little south of Lordington.
> *Map Reference:* SU776094

If you were left a fortune by your father it's unlikely that you would use a considerable part of it to build a folly. Things were different in the eighteenth century, however, and the third Earl of Halifax is said to have lavished all of £10,000 on Racton Tower in the early 1770s. Now in a rather sorry state, it's some 80 feet high and triangular in plan, with a small tower at each corner and a much larger one at the centre. The Earl, whose family home was at Stansted House to the north-west, used it as a look-out. Colourful rumour had it that he entertained excisemen there, befuddling them with drink before lighting flares to tell smugglers that the coast was clear.

EAST DEAN

WILLIAM PEACHEY'S GRAVESTONE

Access: Outside the church, against the east wall.
Map Reference: SU905132

The number of literate people in an out-of-the-way Sussex village three hundred years ago would have been very small, which accounts for some of the oddities on ancient gravestones. The one to William Peachey, who died at East Dean in 1688, is arguably the most delightful of them all. The skull and crossbones at the top are endearingly crude; there is no attempt to complete a word within a single line of text; and the carver must have had the vaguest notion of the phrase *anno domini* and what it signified since he gets it all wrong and omits a date at the foot! The letters *S* and *N* are insribed back-to-front and, the most entertaining of all his mis-spellings, the word *deceased* is transformed by his chisel into something strange and wonderful:

HERE LYETH
THE BODY OF W
ILIAM PEACHE
Y OF EASTDEAN
BLACKSMITHW
HO DISECASED
FEBBRUARYYE
AOM DOM

8

EAST MARDEN

THATCHED WELLHEAD

Access: On a triangle of grass opposite the church.

Map Reference: SU807146

Curiosities can be pretty, too, as exemplified by this unusual village well. The octagonal thatched roof is supported by small tree trunks, and the operating handle of the winding-gear is made from an old cartwheel hub with four spokes and a square rim. Connoisseurs may like to know that there's a double-conical bucket with a narrow top, a single iron reduction gear and a wooden brake on the windlass shaft.

BOXGROVE

CHANTRY CHAPEL

Access: In the church of Boxgrove Priory, sign-posted off the A27 east of Tangmere *Map Reference:* SU908075

The ornate chantry chapel inside the church here was built in 1532 for Thomas, fourth Lord de la Warr, and his wife. This is where masses were to be said for the souls of the founder and his family. Many such chapels were defaced at the Reformation, and Boxgrove's is the only complete one to be found anywhere in Sussex. At the Dissolution, Thomas bought the Benedictine priory in order to save his chantry, but he later moved away and is buried   at   *Broadwater*, Worthing.

The carvings on the chapel's internal pillars depict themes from the French Book of Hours, among them a scene in which boys 'scrump' in a tree while a girl holds her skirt to catch the fruit.

Little survives of the monastic buildings   save   for   the impressive ruins of the monks' three-storey guest house.

HALNAKER

TOWER MILL

Access: By foot up Old Mill Road from Warehead Farm, off the A285.
Map Reference: SU920096

This attractive tower mill is now an empty shell, but its survival was assured in 1958 when the county council undertook to preserve examples of the three main windmill designs: Shipley smock mill and High Salvington post mill were the others. A plaque above the door reveals that 'this ancient landmark' had last been restored in 1934 'by Sir William Bird of Eartham, in memory of his wife.' There was a windmill at Halnaker (pronounced *Hanniker*) at least as far back as 1540, but this one was built around 1750. It has a dummy beehive cap and is hung with russet-red Sussex tiles. The sweeps are permanently fixed to face the south-west.

11

EAST LAVANT

LUCI DE MILDEBI TOMB

Access: In the church.
Map Reference: SU863085

Here's a mystery reminiscent of the 'Who was Cornelius Roetmans?' puzzle at Playden in East Sussex. This stone tomb slab is carved with a simple cross and an exhortation, in Lombardic characters, for the passer-by to pray for the soul of Luci de Mildebi – *PRIEZ: QI: PASSEZ: PAR: ICI: PVR: L'ALME: LVCI: DE: MILDEBI.* There's no date, and we have no clue to Luci's background other than her name and the French inscription. This appears on a piece of Sussex marble – which is not true marble, but a sedimentary stone made of millions of compacted fossil snails *(see Mundham).*

For a similar lettering style, see the tomb of Margaret Camoys at Trotton.

NORTH MUNDHAM

SUSSEX MARBLE FONT

Access: In the church.

Map Reference: SU875022

The font at Mundham is one of the largest in the county, but it's especially interesting for being fashioned from a single block of the material mentioned in the previous entry: Sussex marble. There must have been a good supply available to the mason here, because there are several large Sussex marble graveslabs set into the aisle floor, too.

WEST DEAN

PRESERVED TREE TRUNKS

Access: In the grounds of West Dean College, off the A286.
Map Reference: SU865127

The eccentric Edward James inherited twenty million dollars and the West Dean estate when his father died in 1921. He was a collector and patron of surrealist art (and a friend of Magritte and Dali) but he also spent large sums of money on his follies. The most notable of these were in the Mexican jungle, where he spent nearly forty years building, but never completing, such creations as The Summer Palace with Orange Windows, The House Destined to be a Cinema and The House on Three Floors Which in Fact will have Five. He liked Mexico, he said, because the people didn't treat him as a madman. In the house at West Dean (now an arts and crafts college) he had the footprints of hs wife, the dancer Tilly Losch, woven in white into the carpet. In the garden, which is open to the public during the season, his follies included two beech trunks which – some ten feet high and complete with bracket fungus – were preserved for all time in resin.

WEST WITTERING

TOMB OF BOY BISHOP

> *Access:* In the church.
> *Map Reference:* SZ777985

The crozier and cross on this (Sussex marble) coffin slab suggest that a bishop was buried beneath it. The story is, however, more interesting than that, because this is possibly one of only two tombs of *boy* bishops in the country: the other is at Salisbury. In the middle ages a chorister was chosen to be a kind of mock-bishop for the few weeks leading up to Christmas. He was fully robed and treated just as if he were the real thing. The supposition is the that the poor lad died in office and was therefore given a fitting burial.

WEST WITTERING

ANOTHER SAILOR'S GRAVESTONE

Access: In the churchyard, to the south of the church.
Map Reference: SZ777985

Here's the 'companion piece' to Thomas Burrow's gravestone at Bosham. Both have ships at the top, and the verses differ only in trivial details. Daniel Hack, mariner, who died on February 19, 1770, is given the accolade 'A faithful Servant'. He died at the age of thirty, presumably at sea, but the mason's illustration gives no clue as to the circumstances unless it be the fury of Boreas's blowing in the top right corner. The lettering is worn, but the following transcription is at worst very nearly accurate. It's interesting to compare it with the Burrows stone:

*Tho Boreas's storms and
    Neptune's Waves
Have tos'd me to and fro
In spite of both by God's
    decree
I'm harboured safe below
Where I do now at anchor lie
With many of our Fleet
But once again I must set sail
Our Saviour Christ to meet*

WESTHAMPNETT

OLD SCHOOLHOUSE

Access: By the A27 opposite the entrance to Claypit Lane.
Map Reference: SU883063

The speed of traffic on this main east-west thoroughfare makes a sidelong glance rather hazardous for the driver, but congratulations to whoever decided to register the previous function of this building so appropriately. THE OLD SCHOOL is picked out on coloured tiles while, underneath, the schoolmarm chalks the relevant dates: 1839-1967. That seems to be a dunce's cap on the floor behind her!

WESTHAMPNETT

DOVECOTE

Access: In the grounds of Westhampnett Nursing Home, alongside the A27.
Map Reference: SU882062

Birds flew beneath the rim of the thatch to enter this attractive little dovecote. It's now used as a garden shed, but the nesting holes can still be seen inside.

BOGNOR

ICE HOUSE

Access: Next to the public library in London Road.
Map Reference: SZ936995

Bognor Regis might so easily have become known, instead, as Hothampton! It was a London hatter, Sir Richard Hotham, who first planned to develop the obscure hamlet on this site into a holiday resort. He spent large amounts of money on the place before his death in 1799 and suggested the new name – which somehow never caught on. His grand house lay in what is now known as Hotham Park, and this rather shy domed building of brick and flint, hiding modestly among trees close to the modern shopping centre, provided Sir Richard and his guests with ice during the summer. The ice would be taken from local ponds and lakes in the winter months and packed into the building between insulating layers of straw.

Most large estates had ice houses. Not all those which remain are accessible to the general public, but there are examples at Goodwood, Petworth, Arundel Castle and West Dean in West Sussex, and at Newick Park and Firle in East Sussex.

EASTERGATE

GRANARY

Access: Close to the church at Manor Farm. Follow the signs from the B2233.
Map Reference: SU945051

This magnificent granary building has served the farm for hundreds of years: it's perhaps late Elizabethan or early Stuart in date. The walls are of half-timbered brick, and the building stands on mushroom-shaped staddlestones which keep both damp and the rats at bay.

There's another fine example in the grounds of the Cowdray Ruins at Midhurst.

WESTERGATE

LABOUR IN VAIN

Access: By the A29.
Map Reference: SU944056

This is hardly 'politically correct', but let's give the artist marks for originality when challenged with creating a sign for a pub called *The Labour in Vain.* That piccaninny in the tub is, of course, never going to turn white. As ever, the locals have a story which purports to add further meaning to the sign, suggesting that a former landlord's wife gave birth to a black baby she had more than a little trouble explaining away.

WALBERTON

TWO STRIKING GRAVESTONES

Access: In the churchyard. The Cook stone is on your right as you approach the church. The Rusbridger stone is south of the church.

Map Reference: SU972057

It would be thought bad taste today to illustrate a fatal accident on a gravestone, but there are two remarkable examples at Walberton.

Charles Cook 'lost his life by the fall of a tree on the 20th of March 1767'. The accident is vividly portrayed by the mason: Charles lifeless beneath the great trunk, his tricorn hat beside him, and the woodman with his axe, holding up his hand in horror. We also see a haloed figure in the clouds; angels with trumpets; Old Father Time with his scythe; and a skeleton with an arrow. Quite unforgettable.

Little Ann Rusbridger was killed at the age of eight when a barrel fell from a cart. The date was September 25, 1802, and the scene is vividly depicted on her headstone: large barrel, toppling girl, helpless carter.

BARNHAM

A LANDLORD'S MISCELLANY

Access: On green outside the Murrell Arms, under a copper beech.
Map Reference: SU961044

Mervyn and Daphne Cutten, mine hosts at the Murrell Arms, thought something should be done to enliven what remained of the village green opposite their pub. The result is a gloriously eccentric collection of objects found and created. The Cuttens provided the Barnham village sign and the permanent hopscotch, which is well used by local children. What looks like a bird table is an original pinnacle from the market cross at Chichester while, set into the concrete top (and commemorating 'the liberation of the Falkland Islands, 4 June 1982') are stones from the Murrell River on the Falklands, collected by HMS *Endurance* in 1980. A royalist flavour is much in evidence: the hopscotch has insets to mark the births of Prince William and Prince Harry, and the large slabs beyond the pinnacle (quay stones from the Arundel-Chichester canal) are set out in E formation to honour the Queen Mother's 80th birthday.

MIDHURST

COWDRAY RUINS

> *Access:* Across a causeway from the car park at the Petworth end of the town.
> *Map Reference:* SU891217

A monk's curse is said to have been laid upon the man who bought, and dismantled, Battle Abbey after the Dissolution of the Monasteries: his family line was to perish by fire and water. That was what happened to the descendants of Sir Anthony Browne, but if the Cowdray curse was responsible it took some two and a half centuries to work. In 1793 the family's grand house at Cowdray was destroyed by fire and a week later the eighth Viscount Montague, the last of his line, drowned while attempting to shoot the falls on the Rhine.

Cowdray was built in the reign of Henry VIII (his arms can be seen over one entrance) and Edward VI and Elizabeth I were both entertained here. The remains are open during the season and include a small museum.

In Midhurst itself there are some attractive medieval buildings grouped round the Market Square, reached from the high street via the oddly named Knockhundred Row. The name is supposed to come from the practice of rounding up a hundred men in times of war and other emergencies, but I feel obliged to register my reservations. Was there nowhere else to do the knocking?

EASEBOURNE

BYEPASS BRIDGE

Access: By the A272.
Map Reference: SU896226

On busy polo days at Cowdray, with the road here heavily congested, impatient motorists have been known to take a short-cut under this odd-looking structure. Any why not? As the sign says, motorists not exceeding two tons may use it – at their own risk. The 'byepass bridge' was actually designed for horse traffic.

On the other side of the road is the former site of Easebourne (pronounced Ezbourne) Priory, and some of its buildings are now incorporated into a private house. The priory had a reputation for laxity during the fifteenth century: the Prioress was alleged not only to have been overfond of good food and fancy clothing, but to have given birth to a child.

TROTTON

EARLIEST FEMALE BRASS

Access: In the church.
Map Reference: SU836225

The brass of Margaret, Lady Camoys, on the nave floor at Trotten is a simple one, but it has a claim to fame – it's the oldest brass to be found anywhere in memory of a woman. She died in 1310. The Norman-French inscription in Lombardic lettering has strong similarities with the stone of Luci de Mildebi at *East Lavant,* even to the colons which separate each word: MARGARETE: DE: CAMOYS: GIST: ICI: DEVS: DE: SAALME: EIT: MERCI: AMEN *(Margaret de Camoys lies here. God have mercy on her soul. Amen).*

See also the table tomb in the centre of the chancel, with the brass commemorating Thomas de Camoys and his second wife, Elizabeth Mortimer. She was the widow of Henry Percy, Shakespeare's Harry Hotspur. Thomas de Camoys commanded the left wing of the victorious English army at Agincourt in 1415 and was afterwards made Knight of the Garter. The brass shows him in full armour, holding his wife's hand, and with the Garter below his left knee.

TROTTON

WALL PAINTINGS

Access: In the church.
Map Reference: SU836225

The wall paintings at Trotton date from the early fourteenth century, and there's a detailed Last Judgement on the west wall. This includes the remarkable *Seven Acts of Mercy,* with their details of medieval architecture and fashion. At the centre is the personification of a good man, and the roundels which surround him depict charitable acts such as clothing the naked and feeding the hungry.

MONKTON DOWN

THE DEVIL'S JUMPS

> *Access:* Alongside the South Downs Way. Take a footpath near the Royal Oak at Hooksway.
> *Map Reference:* SU825173

There are 'barrows', or pre-historic burial mounds, all along the South Downs, most of them long since damaged by the plough or ransacked by grave-robbers. The cluster of bell barrows from the Bronze Age known as the Devil's Jumps is among the finest of its kind in southern England. The five main mounds are separated from the sur-rounding ditch by a flat area, or "berm", and two smaller barrows.

Other notable prehistoric sites in West Sussex include Bronze Age barrows on Graffham Down (SU916162), the Bevis's Thumb long barrow (SU 786155), Barkhale neolithic camp (SU976126), Cissbury Ring neolithic flint mines and Iron Age hillfort (TQ136078), Harrow Hill flint mines (TQ082100), The Trundle neolithic camp and Iron Age hillfort (SU877110) and Wolstonbury Hill Iron Age hillfort (TQ284138). The flint mines now appear as a series of slight depressions in the turf.

28

SOUTH HARTING

THE VANDALIAN TOWER

> *Access:* In the grounds of Uppark (up the hill from the gate at the far side of the car park), but visible from B2141, Harting Hill.
> *Map Reference:* SU785182

The terrible fire at Uppark on August 30, 1989, seemed to have destroyed a wonderful house which, in the words of a National Trust guide, was 'a place of stilled richness, enshrining just over a century of the best of English taste, from about 1690, when the house was built, to about 1815, when it entered a sort of embalming sleep.' But no: the decision was taken to spend many millions of pounds on a painstaking restoration so that Uppark should eventually be open to the public once again.

Our curiosity, sadly decayed, lies away from the house atop a hill with wonderful views in all directions. Sir Matthew Fetherstonhaugh built the octagonal gothic folly on Tower Hill, naming it after a projected colony in West Virginia. His son, Sir Harry, inherited Uppark and great wealth in 1774 and had a whale of a time as a young man – travelling, gambling, collecting French furniture, Sevres porcelain and other works of art and entertaining lavishly. His guests, who often included George, the Prince Regent, would carouse in the two-storeyed Vandalian Tower, and it's said that their eating was so excessive that they would afterwards need to be conveyed down the hill to the house in wheel-barrows.

The dairy at Uppark, a little pavilion flooded with light, is where Sir Harry fell in love in his otherwise sober seventies. He was enticed there, it's said, by sweet singing, and he soon afterwards married the singer – his 20-year-old dairymaid, Mary Ann Bullock. They lived together at Uppark for 21 years.

LINCHMERE

THE SEVEN DEADLY SINS

Access: In the church, on the north wall.
Map Reference: SU869309

This fourteenth-century sculpture in hard volcanic rock came to Linchmere from a conventual church in the south of France, but the failings it depicts are, alas, all too universal. The seven monks who lean from their gothic trefoil arches represent the seven deadly sins. Six of them are clean-shaven: the seventh, with a beard and droopy moustache, is Sloth. Their faces are carved from marble.

PETWORTH

LAMP STANDARD

Access: At the junction of North Street and East Street.
Map Reference: SU977217

Street furniture is too often ignored, but this fine cast iron lamp standard of 1851 is a real eye-catcher. Its designer was Sir Charles Barry, architect of the Houses of Parliament. Sir Charles's work in Sussex included St. Peter's Church in Brighton and the parish church at Hurstpierpoint.

The companion East Sussex volume features Victorian licence plates in Eastbourne. One of them, with the letters GCS, is interpreted as Goat Chaise Stand, *but the others are unexplained. Here, to put you out of your misery, are the others –* HCS: *Hackney Carriage Stand;* BCS: *Bath Chair Stand;* MCS: *Motor Charabanc Stand;* SPS: *Saddled Pony Stand;* SDS: *Saddled Donkey Stand;* LPS: *Luggage Porter Stand.*

31

UPPERTON

UPPERTON MONUMENT

Access: In the grounds of Petworth Park, but also visible from the minor road between Tillington and Lurgashall.
Map Reference: SU956233

This stout folly (it's not, in fact, a monument) was built around 1800 in order to be a focus for the view north-west from Petworth House. Tall, plain and built of stone, it's now someone's home – and a most unusual one, too.

TILLINGTON

PITSHILL TOWER

Access: A path runs between laurel hedges close to the eighteenth century house, Pitshill, north-west of Tillington.
Map Reference: SU946230

Probably the hardest to find of any Sussex folly (avoid descending via any of the tempting bridlepaths!), this square three-storey belvedere is now in a sorry state. It has a pyramidal-roofed stair turret, but you certainly shouldn't attempt to climb it. The Mitford family owned Pitshill from 1760 and one of the family was presumably responsible for building the tower.

Note a unique feature of Tillington church – a graceful coronet with four arms curves up from the top of the tower to support a weather-vane. You won't find another one like it.

BIGNOR

ROMAN MOSAICS

Access: Signposted off the minor road between Bignor and West Burton.
Map Reference: SU987147

A farmer's plough turned up the wonders of Bignor back in 1815. The mosaics which are its glory date from the fourth century and are among the finest anywhere in Britain. A large model reveals how the place must have looked in its prime: the villa here was an agricultural centre, and its wealthy Romano-British owners enjoyed baths, fountains and under-floor heating as well as a plethora of fine ornaments and decorations. In creating the mosaics, craftsmen used chalk and limestone for white tesserae, Purbeck marble for blue and grey, and sandstones for reds, oranges and yellows. The head of Medusa is perhaps the most famous of the designs. Our photograph shows a dolphin.

Its mosaics are more varied in quality, but the outstanding Roman-British site in Sussex is Fishbourne Palace, near Chichester, built for the client king Cogidubnus. A stone tablet with a Latin inscription giving Cognidubnus's title is set into the wall of the Council House in North Street, Chichester, close to the spot where it was found in 1723.

BURY

SOME STRANGE CARVINGS

Access: In the main village street.
Map Reference: TQ011132

The weirdest carvings are to be seen on the village stores and the building next door in Bury. Among them are a horse's head, a green man, a seraph and a satyr. Is that Puck sticking out his tongue? And what on earth is that lady with the coronet biting into?

35

BURTON

TABARD TOMB

Access:	In the church in the grounds of St Michaels, Burton Park, east of the A285.
	Map Reference: SU968176

Just as Sussex can boast the earliest brass to a woman *(see Trotton)*, so the county can lay claim to the only brass of a woman wearing a tabard. This is Lady Elizabeth Goring, who died in 1588.

The little church has its walls peppered with texts, paintings and monuments: a wonderful place to discover.

WEST BURTON

A FARMER'S MEMORIAL

> *Access:* Travelling north on the A29, pass the West Burton sign and you'll see a public footpath signed to your left a few hundred yards further on. Cross two stiles: the stone is just to the right off the footpath in a copse.
> *Map Reference:* TQ007137

It's easy to imagine the spirits of Fred and Winifred Hughes hovering about this memorial tablet, if only to enjoy once more the view they must have loved in the days when they worked the farm down below. Fred, we read, *'built the farm you see and never wanted any more, only to be free.'* It was his name alone I saw when I first came across this stone. The later addition is at once sad and delightful: *'Winifred Hughes, his wife, who you could put your arms around.'* I do wish I'd known them!

KIRDFORD

TEMPERANCE TABLET

Access: Not far from the church, on the wall in front of Trerose Cottage.
Map Reference: TQ018266

This attack upon the 'Degradation of Drunkenness' near the centre of Kirdford village has attracted many a story, including that of a supposedly intemperate vicar taken to task by his flock, but the text needs no gloss to be effective. The sign is a replica of the original:

There is no sin which doth more de-face God's image than drunkenness: it disguiseth a person and doth even unman him. Drunkenness makes him have the throat of a fish, the belly of a swine and the head of an ass. Drunkenness is the shame of nature, the extinguisher of reason, the shipwreck of chastity and the murderer of conscience. Drunkenness is hurtful to the body, the cup kills more than the cannon, it causes dropsies, catarrhs, apoplexies, it fills the eye with fire and the legs with water and turns the body into an hospital.

Look out for another sign nearby: dating from 1937, it tells the village story, with references to the Bronze and Iron Ages and the Roman, Saxon, Medieval and Modern periods. In the churchyard is a gravestone recording the terrible year of 1838, when seven villagers were killed in three separate accidents within the space of three months.

NORTHCHAPEL

SHILLINGLEE DEER TOWER

Access: North-east of Northchapel in Shillinglee Park.
Map Reference: SU965315

Not a folly, but even at four storeys high this buff-coloured lookout tower for the deer keeper was not quite tall enough for its wooded site. No doubt, however, it looked dramatic from the house, with its imitation castle keep and the round tower at each corner.

PULBOROUGH

TOAT MONUMENT

Access: Toat is signposted west off the A29 north of Pulborough. Follow Blackgate Lane, and keep on the road marked No Through Road. You'll see it (on private land belonging to Toat House) up on your left.
Map Reference: TQ050216

The Toat Monument, a castellated octagonal tower some 40 feet high, is a memorial to Samuel Drinkald who took a fatal fall from his horse in 1823. The tower was built four years later.

STOPHAM

MEDIEVAL BRIDGE

Access: Just south of the A283 west of Pulborough.
Map Reference: TQ030184

Now that it has been bypassed, it's difficult to remember that this beautiful but very narrow medieval bridge was busy with traffic (one-way and controlled by lights) until the late 1980s. It was built over the Arun in 1423 to replace the old ferry and is the most beautiful of its kind in Sussex, with refuges, or passing places, along its length. Its central arch was raised in 1822 so that masted vessels could sail upriver to join the Wey and Arun Canal.

HARDHAM

MEDIEVAL WALL PAINTINGS

Access: In the church.
Map Reference: TQ037175

The wall paintings at Hardham are not only among the earliest, but the best, medieval wall paintings to survive in England. Elsewhere you see fragments: here the entire plan of the original artists remains virtually intact. There are some forty individual subjects, including this magnificent Adam and Eve in the chancel. Adam is pointing towards Eve, who takes the apple from the winged serpent coiled in a tree. There's something unusual to look out for here: the artist gave his work the effect of a textile hanging by suggesting that it was suspended by loops from a rail above.

Stylistically, the paintings suggest a date of about 1100, with similarities to the Bayeux Tapestry. The tall, slender figures are in the Anglo-Saxon tradition. Apart from Adam and Eve, there's a long 'christological' cycle (from the birth of Jesus to the crucifixion) and various judgement and apocalyptic themes. One scene shows St George in battle, and the church guide suggests that this may represent the Battle of Antioch in 1098. The church, now St Botolph's, was originally dedicated to St. George.

See also the medieval wall paintings at Clayton, Coombes and Plumpton. These three churches and Hardham are thought to have been decorated by the same workshop, because of the similarity of technique, style and subject-matter.

CONEYHURST

THE BLUE IDOL

Access: Signposted from the A272 between Coneyhurst and Coolham.
Map Reference: TQ108232

William Penn, the Quaker founder of Pennsylvania, used to walk the few miles from his home at Warminghurst to speak at meetings held in this converted farmhouse. He would have climbed those steps and, no doubt, sat on that elders' bench before addressing the gathered Society of Friends: our photograph is taken from the small gallery above. The Quakers came here in 1691, at a time of persecution (*see Twineham*). Between 1793 and 1869 the building lay idle and was colour-washed in blue, which (improbable though it sounds) is the best explanation yet suggested for its present name. Quaker meetings are still held here, but part of the building now serves as a guest house.

LOXWOOD

COKELERS' CHAPEL

Access: Along Spy Lane to the north of the village.
Map Reference: TQ042319

John Sirgood would be sad to know that the Cokelers have gone, but he would perhaps derive some comfort from seeing that their chapel remains a place of worship. Sirgood was a shoemaker who, divinely guided in a dream, came to Sussex from London in 1850 and began to preach from his cottage in Loxwood. His Society of Dependants (commonly known as the Cokelers) had two thousand members by the time of his death in 1885, with several chapels in the surrounding area and shops run on cooperative lines in Loxwood, Northchapel and Warnham, as well as at Shamley Green in Surrey and at Norwood in South London. In some villages nearly half the inhabitants were members, sharing a belief that, having chosen to follow Christ rather than succumb to the temptations of the flesh, they could do no wrong. They dressed in black and rejected a large number of life's pleasures, among them alcohol, tobacco, secular books, music and flowers in the home. Marriage was allowed but rather frowned upon, so that it's not altogether surprising that the sect should have eventually died out towards the end of the twentieth century. Sirgood and his followers lie in unmarked graves in the burial ground which adjoins the chapel.

ARUNDEL

HIORNE TOWER

> *Access:* By foot from Arundel Park, following the path round Swanbourne Lake then climbing steeply; or along a track from a point to the west of the parish church.
>
> *Map Reference:* TQ013081

A sad case of might-have-been. The architect Francis Hiorne ran up this folly for the eleventh Duke of Norfolk in 1787 as a 'specimen': he hoped that it would win him the contract for re-building the castle. Alas, Hiorne died two years later at the age of 45.

In front of the tower (once lived in, but now derelict) is an ancient urn which, an inscription tells us, was 'found in the museum at Sevastopol on the fall of the place before the Allied forces by sea and land, September the 8th, 1855, after one of the most memorable sieges upon record'.

ARUNDEL

TWO CHURCHES IN ONE

Access: St. Nicholas' church – but the Fitzalan chapel may be entered only from the castle grounds.
Map Reference: TQ016074

It's a very long walk from the nave to the chancel in Arundel's parish church: allow yourself a good half an hour. Be prepared, too, for a change of religion: from Anglican to Roman Catholic.

This curiosity can be traced back to the fourteenth century, when an iron grille was first installed to allow a college of secular canons exclusive use of the eastern end of the church for their worship. In suppressing the college, Henry VIII sold it to the Earl of Arundel along with all its possessions – including the chancel. During the Civil War the Parliamentary forces did a great deal of damage to the church, as well as to the castle. Subsequent repairs left the chancel completely blocked off, with services held in the nave. Much later, in 1880, the then vicar attempted to get a legal ruling that everything should come under his jurisdiction. He lost, the High Court acknowledging the ownership of the (Roman Catholic) Dukes of Norfolk.

The Roman Catholic cathedral, a landmark high on the other side of the road from the parish church, was a gift to local Catholics from the fifteenth Duke. The architect was J.A. Hansom, better known as the inventor of the Hansom Cab.

ARUNDEL

TRADERS' SIGNS

Access: In the High Street.
Map Reference: TQ018072

There was a time when each trade had its own recognisable sign to catch the illiterate customer's eye. These buildings date from only 1890 (a drainpipe proclaims the date) but two of them follow tradition. The gable with chequerboard design advertises a gunsmith, while the anvil atop another signifies that this was an ironmonger's shop. Since Arundel is a traditionally-minded town, it's only fitting that an ironmonger should still be in residence at the sign of the anvil more than a century later!

BURPHAM

SPINNING JENNY

Access:　　In the George & Dragon restaurant.
Map Reference: TQ039089

What kind of game would you expect to play with this Spinning Jenny, mounted on the dining room ceiling at the George & Dragon? Apparently revolving dials of this kind were once quite common in the county's public houses. The ten segments of this sturdy example are marked with Roman numerals, the *four* being written *1111* as on traditional clock faces. Perhaps, as has been suggested, the customers would once 'twizzle' to decide who should buy the next round, though the ale must have tasted pretty sour in the mouth of a man whose number came up too often. That is, at least, a more likely explanation that the most common one you'll hear: that smugglers used it to divide their booty. The sheer injustice of it at the end of a hard, dark night evading the excisemen would surely have led to vicious blood-letting. May one suggest, more prosaically, that the spinning jenny simply provided a pub's clientele with humble sport (whether for money or not) before the age of snooker, television and one-armed bandits?

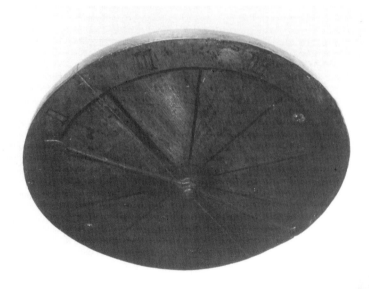

SLINDON

EARLIEST WOODEN EFFIGY

Access: In the church.
Map Reference: SU961084

Here's another of those Sussex one-offs: the only wooden effigy to be found anywhere in the county. Five feet long and made of oak, it represents Sir Anthony St Leger, who died in 1539. In his will he asked to be interred in the church before the picture of Our Lady. Neither the picture nor Sir Anthony's tomb still exists, and his effigy was removed from the chancel to its present position when the organ chamber was installed. He's dressed in plate armour, proud codpiece and all, with his head resting on his helmet.

Sussex can also claim the oldest wooden graveyard memorial anywhere – in the church at Sidlesham. It's an oak beam which was once erected over a grave in the churchyard. Lettering on two faces shows that it once marked the last resting place of Thomas Greenwood, who died in 1658. Its survival is something of a miracle, because at one time it was used to repair a gatepost in the village. Someone rescued it and, after a spell at Chichester Museum, it was restored to the church.

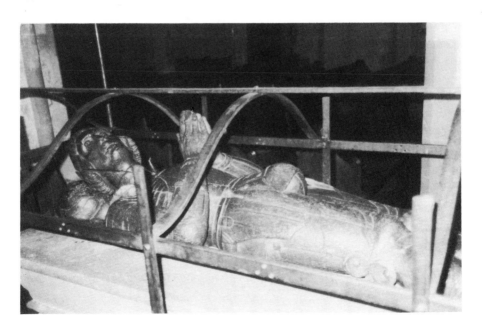

SLINDON

NORE FOLLY

Access: After passing Slindon College take an unmarked right turn down towards Courthill Farm. At the foot of the hill fork left beside a pond along an unmade track. After a few hundred yards a footpath takes you up the hill.

Map Reference: TQ955095

Like many a folly, this one is more handsome from a distance than at close quarters. It's made of flint and was built by the Kemp family during the latter half of the eighteenth century. It had a function other than to strike a pose in the landscape, however. Behind one pillar you'll see a ring of flint footings. Here there was once a thatched luncheon room, where the Earl and Countess of Newburgh would take their guests for refreshment while out shooting.

The folly is maintained by the National Trust, which owns the 3,500 acre Slindon Estate.

POLING

'WORLD IS A ROUND THING' GRAVESTONE

Access: In the church porch.
Map Reference: TQ047047

Whether Alice, wife of Robert Woolldridge, was herself rich or poor we don't know, but her gravestone of 1740 points an undeniable moral in rough-hewn verse:

The World is a round thing
And full of crooked streets.
Death is a market place
Where all Men meets.
If Life was a thing
That money could buy
The Rich would live
And the Poor would dye.

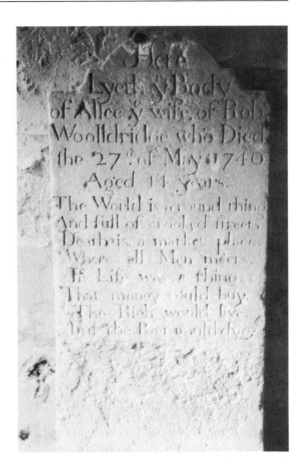

POLING

POOR BOX

Access: In the church.
Map Reference: TQ047047

This is the only surviving ancient poor-box in West Sussex. It's bound in iron, and on the top plates are the letters *Rt de H I C of A* and the date *1285.* The initials are thought to stand for Robert de Hastings and his wife Isabella, Countess of Arundel. The letters and date *ICT 1797* appear on plates lower down.

Above the box is a carved stone which must surely have embarrassed the mason until the end of his days: *PRAYE REMEBER THE POORE.* But, in an era of patchy literacy, perhaps nobody minded very much.

Not that all such errors are ancient. See inside the porch of South Malling church at Lewes (where the founder of Harvard university was married to a local girl) for a confident modern mis-spelling of 'Massachusetts'.

TORTINGTON

BEAKHEAD ORNAMENTATION

Access: In the Church.
Map Reference: TQ003050

The weird collection of start-eyed creatures clustered around the chancel arch at Tortington was probably picked out in paint by its Norman creators, in which case standing in the nave for worship must have been an uncomfortable, not to say frightening, experience. This style of work is known as beakhead ornamentation, since several of the grotesques clasp the roll moulding in their beaks. The only example in Sussex anything like it is at *Broadwater* church, Worthing.

YAPTON

SHOULDER OF MUTTON & CUCUMBERS

Access: B2233 just east of B2132 junction and church.
Map Reference: SU977033

There are Shoulder of Mutton pubs throughout the country, but surely no other with the cucumbers, too! Was this once a recognised gastronomic combination?

It was at this pub that a notorious case of wife-selling occurred around the turn of the century. A rat-catcher named White, who lodged here, fancied the wife of a thatcher called Marley. A bargain was struck at the bar: the rat-catcher took Mrs. Marley, the children and the furniture in return for 7s 6d and a quart of beer.

CLIMPING

CRUSADERS' CHEST

Access: In the church.
Map Reference: TQ003026

When Pope Innocent III was promoting the fifth crusade (1218-1221) he ordered that boxes or chests should be installed in every parish church for the collection of arms, equipment and money. With its intricate carving of rosettes and arches, this is a particularly fine example of one of those thirteenth-century Crusaders' Chests. Although the original locks have disappeared, some of the iron bands and chains remain on the back.

Note, outside the church, the ornate Norman west door with its chevron and dog-tooth designs and the tower window enclosed by chevron moulding. This is a highly unusual feature.

BROADWATER

MISERICORDS

> *Access:* In the church.
> *Map Reference:* TQ146044

It's relatively unusual to find misericords in parish churches, but there are several in the chancel here. The infirm would use them to rest against when they were supposed to be standing during long and tiring services. The woodcarvers often amused themselves no end, decorating parts of seats which couldn't easily be seen with animals and grotesques. The work at Broadwater is restrained, but the faces on the bench-ends certainly have character.

Other misericords can be seen in West Sussex at Chichester Cathedral; at St Mary's Hospital Almshouses, also in Chichester; in the Fitzalan chapel at Arundel; and, close to Broadwater, at the parish church of West Tarring. In East Sussex, visit Etchingham.

SHOREHAM

THE MARLIPINS

Access: In the High Street.
Map Reference: TQ215050

Most buildings which survive from the early middle ages had a religious or military function, so The Marlipins (now housing a local maritime museum) is something of a rarity. This sturdy building is Norman in origin, though the chequerboard facade of flint and stone dates from the fourteenth century. It's thought to have been the port's first customs house: barrels of brandy and wine would have been stored in its undercroft.

KINGSTON BUCI

ANCHORITE'S CELL

Access: Take Kingston Lane from the A259 and then the first turning left.
Map Reference: TQ235053

Look closely at that pillar and you'll see an oblique mark which is the trace of an ancient lean-to roof. In the days before that door was built an anchorite was walled up here: the small aperture giving on to the chancel was his one means of contact with his fellow man and woman.

Being walled up for life wasn't uncommon in the Middle Ages. The north side of the church was usually chosen (as here) because it was colder – so demanding more faith and fortitude.

For other traces of such cells visit Boxgrove Priory and St. Anne's, Lewes (the latter featured in the East Sussex companion to this volume).

SHOREHAM BEACH

RAILWAY CARRIAGE HOME

> *Access:* In Old Fort Road.
> *Map Reference:* TQ219045

Shoreham Beach still has its small houseboat community, but little remains of the 'bungalow town' that existed here (and at several points along the Sussex coast) until the Army cleared the foreshore during the second world war. Many of the ramshackle homes and holiday retreats weren't bungalows at all, but were improvisations which used whatever materials came to hand: bus bodies, tramcars, railway carriages. Here's a doughty survivor from those times, *LB SC* standing for *London Brighton & South Coast Railway.*

See also West Front Road at Pagham for a number of ingenious conversions.

SOMPTING

RHENISH HELM

Access: Clearly visible just off the A27.
Map Reference: TQ162056

The tower of Sompting church was built decades before the Norman Conquest and it's the only remaining English example of the so-called Rhenish Helm. Its original Saxon timbers are still intact. The arch, inside the tower, is a noted example of Saxon architecture – 'built', as the church guide says, 'by men who had seen Roman arches still standing in Sussex'.

In 1154 Sompting church was granted to the Knights Templars, the crusading order. They rebuilt it, adding the north and south transepts as chapels for the use of their own members. The order was suppressed early in the fourteenth century.

For other examples of Templar influence, see the churches at Shipley (built for the order around 1250), Bramber and Washington.

HIGHDOWN HILL

THE MILLER'S TOMB

> *Access:* A footpath runs west from the car park by Highdown Gardens, signposted off the A259.
> *Map Reference:* TQ096044

The eccentric miller John Olliver was more than well prepared for his death. He kept his coffin under the bed for all of 27 years before he died (in 1793, aged 84), and he'd planned his funeral service in great detail: the mourners were all to wear bright clothing, with the burial service read by a young girl. He apparently left money for the maintenance of his tomb high on the Downs, but a great deal of the lettering has now been worn away by the weather. The clearest is at the western end where the Biblical quotation *The fear of GOD is the beginning of wisdom/But to keep his commandments is holiness to the LORD* overarches bas-relief figures of Death and Time. Beneath them is a sonnet:

Death, why so fast? pray stop your hand,
And let my glass run out its sand:
As neither Death nor Time will stay,
Let us improve the present day.
Why start you at that skeleton?
'Tis your own picture which you shun.
Alive it did resemble thee
And thou when dead like that shall be:
But tho' Death must have his will,
Yet old Time prolongs the date,
Till the measure we shall fill
That's allotted us by Fate.
When that's done, then TIME and DEATH
Both agree to take our breath!

CLAPHAM

CASTELLATED TOLL HOUSE

Access: By the A280 between Findon and Clapham.
Map Reference: TQ101075

What a strange building to stand all alone beside a quiet country road! This small castle, which sadly doesn't even begin to evoke thoughts of fair maidens and knightly deeds, is the Long Furlong toll house. It was built in 1820, and the arched recess in the facade was designed for the toll board with its list of charges.

WASHINGTON

CHANCTONBURY RING

> *Access:* A footpath begins by the Franklands Arms off the A283 at Washington.
> *Map Reference:* TQ139121

Back in 1760, while still in his teens, Charles Goring decided to plant a clump of trees on the top of Chanctonbury Hill. Though the 'ring' properly refers to the earthworks of the Iron age hill-fort around the summit, for most people it means these trees – sadly battered though they were by the great storm of October 1987. Goring, whose family owned the vast estate here, wrote a poem some 70 years later, recalling his youthful hope to see the hilltop 'in all its beauty dress'd'. Lucky man:

> *That time's arrived; I've had my wish,*
> *And lived to eighty-five . . .*

Cissbury Ring, a little more than two miles to the south (TQ140080), is the most impressive of the fortifications built along the Downs during the Iron Age. At this site you can also see evidence of the neolithic flint mines which were once sunk to a depth of fifty feet, with cramped galleries running from a central shaft. The mines can now be seen as a series of pock-marks in the turf.

STEYNING

WAPPINGTHORN WATER TOWER

Access: Track through Wappington Farm off the B2135 north of Steyning.
Map Reference: TQ169137

This helter-skelter architectural design, the work of Max Ayrton in 1928, is thoroughly practical. The summer house at the top of the 80ft structure can be reached only from the outside because the grade two listed tower is full of water. It holds, in fact, ten thousand gallons, and is the main supply to the farm in which it stands.

The water tower is well hidden from the road, but the main farm building itself is of a whimsical piece with it.

BRAMBER

CASTLE RUINS

Access: From the roundabout at the western end of the village.
Map Reference: TQ186107

It may be hard to believe at first glance, but Bramber was one of the five great castles built by the Normans to defend Sussex against attacks from the sea – the others were Arundel, Lewes, Pevensey and Hastings. This one is in the sorriest state. After long periods of neglect, punctuated by military occupation during the Civil War, it was eventually used as a quarry for local road building. The castle was built on a massive natural mound: from the stunted remains of the flint ramparts you can see for miles across the valley of the river Adur, which was once navigable as far upriver as Bramber. At the centre of the site is a large, wooded mound which was once fortified. The tall finger of masonry which survives was part of the keep.

Inside the church, close to the castle remains, look out for the carvings on the capitals of the tower arch. The work on the north side, crudely done, is said to be one of only three examples of Norman eleventh century figured sculpture in England. On the south side, beneath another early carving, is supposed fourteenth century work which includes a staff surmounted by a Maltese cross. This is thought to be a sign of the church's association with the Knights Templars (see Sompting), who had their house at the end of the village where St. Mary's House now stands.

BRAMBER

LEPERS' WINDOWS

> *Access:* St. Botolph's Church, south east of Bramber. Take a minor road from the roundabout at the western end of the village.
> *Map Reference:* TQ195093

Low-side windows in church chancels were often installed so that people refused admittance for some reason might nevertheless see the altar through the 'squint' and worship from afar. The term "lepers' windows" is perhaps used too freely, but there's a good reason for believing that this was the function of the two low windows at St Botolph's (one on the north wall, the other on the south): in medieval times a village flourished here, with its own wharf alongside a wide estuary, and the St. Mary Magdalene Hospital for Lepers was situated about a mile away.

SULLINGTON

TITHE BARN

Access: At Manor Farm, off the A283 east of Storrington.
Map Reference: TQ098138

The finest of its kind in West Sussex, this tithe barn of tarred weatherboarding under a tiled roof is all of 115ft long. It's close to the church, which would once have gathered here a tenth of what its local tenant farmers produced.

To inspect it at close quarters (it has aisles and a braced tie-beam roof inside) you need permission from the farm.

For a magnificent example in East Sussex, see the Alciston *entry in our companion volume.*

DIAL POST

KNEPP CASTLE

Access: Alongside the A24 north of Dial Post.
Map Reference: TQ164209

King John was among the notables who visited Knepp Castle when it was used chiefly as a hunting lodge by the de Braose family. He kept some two hundred greyhounds here for hunting deer. After 1216 it was no longer fortified and it gradually became a ruin, the stone being used for road building (a fate which also befell the principal de Braose castle at *Bramber*). Now, despite sporting a jaunty weather-vane, it's a rather pathetic fragment.

WARMINGHURST

BOX PEWS

Access: In the church.
Map Reference: TQ118169

The Victorians improved, by their own lights, so many of our Sussex churches that it's rare to find an interior like the one at Warminghurst. The Protestant Reformation had seen a shift in the focus of worship from the altar to the pulpit, with a greater participation by the congregation and services conducted in English: the First English Prayer Book was introduced in 1549. The influential High Church movement of the nineteenth century, by contrast, sought a return to a medieval aura of mystery, with an emphasis on ritual rather than preaching. Zealous restorers tore out furniture which they saw as at best irrelevant. Warminghurst is one of only about 140 English 'prayer book' interiors to have survived. It has late eighteenth century box pews, a three-decker pulpit of the same period and a chancel screen with a tympanum decorated with the arms of Queen Anne.

For other West Sussex examples of 'prayer book' furnishings and fittings see Up Marden; St. John, Chichester; and the little church in the grounds of Parham Park, near Storrington. In East Sussex: Ashburnham, Glynde and Penhurst, near Battle.

ASHURST

VAMPING HORN

Access: In the church.
Map Reference: TQ176164

Before the days of organs, churches depended for their music on whatever local talent they could find – and whatever instruments. Vamping horns were apparently used as a kind of backing and perhaps gave the initial pitch: the *OED* glosses *vamp* as 'to improvise or extemporize (an accompaniment, tune etc.)' and a note in Ashurst Church tells us that 'vamping came to mean supporting others in the band.' There are only seven such horns anywhere in England, and all the others are trumpet-shaped: this one is best described as a broken cone. Another unique feature is the framework of wires inside, possibly for resonance. The vamping horn, beautifully restored, has the date 1770 on it, the maker's name (Palmer) and the Biblical quotation *Praise Him upon the strings and pipe.*

HENFIELD

THE CAT HOUSE

> *Access:*   Pinchnose Green, off Church Street.
> *Map Reference:* TQ213163

Birds are killed by cats every day, unfortunately, but one act of feline rapacity has never been forgotten in well over a hundred years. This strangely decorated house is – or so the story goes – a constant reminder that a canary owned by the local joiner, Bob Ward, was savaged by a cat belonging to Nathaniel Woodard (died 1891), the founder of the group of public schools which includes Lancing, Ardingly and Hurstpierpoint Colleges. Ward, who must have been an unforgiving type, installed a contraption of metal cats with bells, which he jangled loudly every time Woodard walked past. They were later attached to the cottage walls.

Pinchnose Green, incidentally, got its name from the trade formerly practised here: it was the site of a tannery.

TWINEHAM

QUAKER BURIAL GROUND

> *Access:* In the churchyard, on your left close to the entrance.
> *Map Reference:* TQ253200

That stone in the middle foreground was one of four which marked out a highly unusual area of the graveyard of the parish church at Twineham: the other three seem to have been removed. The stone on the left explains that this is a burial ground belonging to the Society of Friends (or Quakers) and purchased in 1694. Fifty-six burials were recorded, the last in 1732. Yet the seventeenth century was a time of persecution for the Quakers, many of them being jailed for their opposition to the established religion of what they derisively termed the 'steeple houses'.

What happened at Twineham is that the vicar's daughter married a Quaker, and he offered this piece of land to the Friends so that she shouldn't be buried in unconsecrated ground. Although they loathed the tithing system, they agreed to pay a shilling a year for the plot on condition that the church, in turn, paid 1s 6d for using the grass as animal fodder. The rector still pays his dues at a ceremony by the burial ground.

The church building itself is notable for being one of only three in Sussex to be built of Tudor brick. The others are at Egdean, near Petworth (though most of the brickwork disappeared in a restoration) and at East Guldeford, near Rye in East Sussex.

FULKING

A DOWNLAND SPRING

Access: Outside the Shepherd and Dog pub.
Map Reference: TQ247114

The pretty minor road that runs under the Downs past the Shepherd and Dog keeps to the spring-line, and water gushes vigorously from the chalk here. On the side of the storage house just below the pub is an attractive tiled plaque. The Victorian tile-setter managed to put three of his Ss upside down in reproducing this fitting Biblical text: *He sendeth springs into the valleys which run among the hills. Oh that man would praise the Lord for His goodness.*

Up the hill on the left is a fountain with a red marble tablet. This was installed in honour of a man whose friends in the village had asked for his knowledge and influence in getting them a permanent water supply. He was none other than the art critic John Ruskin.

CLAYTON

CASTELLATED RAILWAY TUNNEL

> *Access:* By the A273, close to the Jack and Jill pub.
> *Map Reference:* TQ298141

As if it wasn't strange enough to create this railway tunnel in the likeness of a castle (battlemented turrets, arrowslits and all) the authorities later decided to build a cottage on top. The inhabitants have long since failed to notice the noise of the trains which pass below. When the London-Brighton line was opened in 1841 the tunnel was lit by gas. The trains were, of course, powered by steam: by the side of the A273, towards Brighton, you can see the necessary brick ventilation shafts and the spoil heaps produced in their construction.

In the church, across the road in Underhill Lane, are some fine medieval wall paintings (see Hardham) *with scenes of the Last Judgement, Christ in Glory and the Fall of Satan.*

CLAYTON

JACK AND JILL WINDMILLS

Access: Signposted from the A273 between Clayton and Hassocks.
Map Reference: TQ303134

These are the most famous of the Sussex windmills, standing in stark and handsome contrast high on the Downs. Jack, the black one, is a tower mill: it's brick-built and the cap and sweeps turn to face the wind. Jill, painted white, fully restored and open to the public, is a post mill: the whole structure revolves around a single massive wooden pillar.

For a lovely example of the third kind of windmill, the smock mill, visit Shipley. The cap turns, as on a tower mill, but the body of the mill is wooden and shaped like a shepherd's smock.

PYECOMBE

TAPSELL GATE

Access: Church signposted off the A273 near the junction with the A23.
Map Reference: TQ292126

Not all shepherd's crooks were alike, and those fashioned at Pyecombe were known for their distinctive shape. Here's one on the tapsell gate at the entrance to the churchyard. The old forge is downhill from the church. Our companion volume for East Sussex refers to a group of tapsell gates in the Eastbourne area and carries a photograph of the one at Friston: their distinguishing feature is that they turn on a central pillar.

For another tapsell gate in West Sussex, visit Coombes, near Lancing.

SADDLESCOMBE

DONKEY WHEEL

> *Access:*   The hamlet lies off the Devil's Dyke road south east from Poynings. The
> donkey wheel is in a field beyond the farmyard.
> *Map Reference:* TQ273116

One donkey or two men were required to turn this wheel, which raised water from a well about 175ft. deep. It took twenty eight turns to raise the wooden bucket, and the water was then tipped into lead-lined cisterns. The wheel dates from perhaps the end of the eighteenth century and was in use until around 1910. It's in a small timber building and is now maintained by Brighton Council.

HORSTED KEYNES

CRUSADER'S HEART BURIAL

> *Access:* In the church.
> *Map Reference:* TQ383286

This monument to a thirteenth century knight is only 27 inches long, which is why it's commonly held to be a heart burial. When a knight died on one of the Crusades his body would be buried in that far-off country while his heart was sent back to rest in his homeland. This crusader may have been one of the Keynes (pronounced 'Canes') family which has given the village the second part of its name.

How did young Henry Pigott come to be buried nine months before he was born? A monument in the chancel shows that William and Jane Pigott had four sons, none of whom survived beyond his teens. Henry, we read, was born on December 30, 1715, and was buried on March 7, 1715. The explanation is that in those days the New Year began on March 25: it wasn't until 1752 (when the Gregorian calendar replaced the Julian) that the English adopted January 1 as the year's starting date . Poor little Henry, then, lived for two months and a few days.

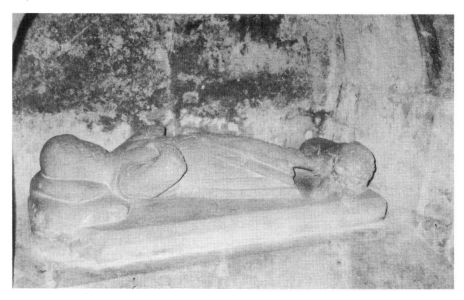

LINDFIELD

HORSE GIN

Access: In the back garden of the Red Lion in the High Street.
Map Reference: TQ347254

This old structure – an octagonal slated roof supported by wooden pillars – once housed a horse-gin. Since the gin was used to draw well water for a brewery, it's perhaps fitting that it should be found in the garden of the Red Lion. The truth is, however, that it was moved to its present site (from a yard not far away) after it was on the point of collapse and the parish council decided to rescue it. The brick paved track for the horse was left where it was, on the orders of the county archaeologist, and can be seen behind the Linden Tree Pub almost immediately opposite the Red Lion.

At Old Place, at the top of the High Street, the iron cage of another horse-gin stands above the well. Peer from the lane behind the church and you may be able to make out the brick paving here, too.

HORSHAM

MUSLIM TOMBSTONE

> *Access:* In the churchyard of St. Mary the Virgin, immediately on your right as
> you approach from The Causeway.
> *Map Reference:* TQ171303

Tombstones traditionally face east in Christian churchyards, so why the flagrant breaking
of the code here? Helena Bennett was a Muslim from the Middle East who, nominally at
least, became a Catholic on marrying her English husband. He later deserted her. Although
her tomb was given a stone cross, it was dug at the 'wrong' angle to spare her the
posthumous indignity of being thought a Christian.

CRAWLEY

RACEHORSE BANDSTAND

Access: In Queen's Square.
Map Reference: TQ270367

This elegant Victorian bandstand has travelled. It has, moreover, known a few special occasions in its time. Now it sits among the concrete and plate glass in Crawley's main shopping precinct, but its previous home was at the old Gatwick racecourse – closed down years ago to make way for the international airport. And those special occasions? During the first world war, when the famous Aintree racecourse in Liverpool was closed, the Grand National was run at Gatwick.

WORTH

SAXON CHURCH

Access::   Signposted off the B2036 south of Worth.
Map Reference: TQ302363

Among the largest and best preserved pre-Conquest churches in England, Worth dates from somewhere between 950 and 1050. The Victorians rebuilt the unusual apse you see, but on the original plinth and using the existing stone. The two transepts, the main arches and the greater part of the nave walls are original Saxon work. The chancel arch is massive – uniquely so in a church of this age.

In September 1986, while the roof timbers were being treated, a fierce fire broke out. The main building was saved, but the church was later given a new roof, a new floor of French limestone and new pews. Among the older fittings are a pulpit of 1577 which has inscriptions in Low German (it was bought from a London antiques dealer in 1841 by the then rector), and a gallery at the west end: *This Gallerie is the gift of Anthony Lynton, late Rector of the Parish, who deceased the XV day of June Anno Domini 1610.*

ST. LEONARD'S FOREST

HAMMER PONDS

Access:: At Bucks Head, alongside the minor road which runs from the A281 south of Horsham to Ashfold Crossways on the A279 south west of Handcross.
Map Reference: TQ216292, TQ219289

Hawkins Pond and Hammer Pond sit side by side here, and the latter name is the give-away. Throughout the Weald of Sussex you'll find these now-tranquil sheets of water which were once the source of power for a thriving iron industry. The Romans had been the first to exploit the iron (traces of their 'bloomeries' can still be found) but more sophisticated techniques later made Sussex a centre for the production of armaments, bells, graveslabs, firebacks and tools from the sixteenth century. The dense forests of the Weald provided wood for charcoal, while the water drove giant bellows in the blast furnaces and huge hammers in the forges. Names of woods, ponds and houses which include the words 'hammer' or "furnace' usually indicate one of these sites. The last iron furnace in Sussex (at Ashburnham, near Battle) closed in 1820, though the boom was over long before then.

DRAGONS GREEN

GRAVESTONE IN PUB GARDEN

Access:: Take a minor road off the A272 east of Coolham.
Map Reference: TQ140235

A sad tale with a strange result. Walter Budd, an albino and an epileptic, lived with his parents at the George and Dragon pub. He was, it seems, treated unkindly by some of the local people. In 1893 he was accused of a trivial theft and, a few days after his twenty-sixth birthday, he drowned himself. Walter's parents, angry as well as grief-stricken, ordered the following inscription for his tombstone in Shipley churchyard: *May God forgive those who forgot their duty to him who was just and afflicted.* This criticism was ill-received and the vicar refused to accept the memorial. Where else, then, could the Budds place it but in front of their pub? It stands there to this day, making its protest far more effectively than if it had been tucked away in the churchyard.

WEST GRINSTEAD

FARM NAMES ON PEWS

> *Access:*   The church is signposted south of the B2135.
> *Map Reference:* TQ171207

You couldn't sit where you liked in West Grinstead church in days gone by. The names of dozens of surrounding farms and houses appear in (beautifully maintained) early nineteenth century lettering on the pews, and nearly all of them can still be traced. These, at the front of the church, were for men only: women and children sat at the back, where the named pews have since gone. Extremely orderly, but one's absence from a service must have been conspicuous.

For another example of this proprietorial spirit see Shermanbury church, near Henfield, which has named box pews.

WARNHAM

MICHAEL TURNER'S GRAVE

Access::   In the churchyard, south of the church.
Map Reference: TQ159337

Ah, they don't write them like they used to! Michael Turner was not only the clerk and sexton at Warnham Church for fifty years but its leading musician, too. (Some of the ancient church instruments can still be seen inside). He always wore a white smock frock with a red handkerchief, tie and breeches, and he sported an old-fashioned beaver high hat on Sundays. He died just before Christmas 1885 at the age of 89, and – as his gravestone make clear in decidedly chirpy verse – he went the way any musician would like to go, while in full spate:

His duty done, beneath this stone
Old Michael lies at rest.
His rustic rig, his song, his jig
Were ever of the best.

With nodding head the choir he led,
That none should start too soon.
The second, too, he sang full true,
His viol played the tune.

And when at last his age had passed
One hundred less eleven
With faithful cling to fiddle string
He sang himself to heaven.

EAST GRINSTEAD

GUINEA PIG PUB SIGN

Access::   Along Quarry Rise, off Holtye Road, close to the Queen Victoria Hospital.   *Map Reference:* TQ401395

This pub sign isn't the easiest to decipher. That *is* one of the little furry creatures at the centre, but why the wings and the flames? The proximity of the Queen Victoria Hospital is the clue. During the second world war experimental plastic surgery was carried out here on pilots and other servicemen who'd received severe facial injuries. They were happy to be known as 'guinea pigs' – and they still return to Sussex for reunions.

EAST GRINSTEAD

WHERE 'GOOD KING WENCESLAS' WAS WRITTEN

> *Access:* Sackville College, Lewes Road.
> *Map Reference:* TQ397380

This is the study in which the Reverend John Mason Neale, scholar, historian, linguist and author, sat down to compose a Christmas carol which is known to every man, woman and child in the land: *Good King Wenceslas.* He also wrote a great many hymns that will be known to any regular worshipper.

Neale, a highly controversial character, was warden of Sackville College from 1846 until his early death twenty years later. He was a prime mover in the High Church movement and was forbidden to preach in the chapel here after being reported to the bishop for erecting a rood cross. This smacked rather too aggressively of Romanism, and passions ran so high that Neale was physically assaulted.

The College (built by the Earls of Dorset for the local poor and today a home for eighteen elderly people) is open to the public during the season. Neale's study and the rood cross can be seen. Look out, too, for the huge and intricate lock on the chapel door (see p.viii), and for a sign which reminded the early inmates whom they had to thank: 'I pray God bles my Lord of Dorset and my Ladie and al their posteritie Ano Do 1619.'